# The BIBLE Project Book

## CONTENTS

| | | | |
|---|---|---|---|
| What is the Bible? | 2 | Two famous Kings | 18 |
| The Bible Lands | 4 | The books of wisdom | 20 |
| How people lived in Bible times | 6 | The Prophets | 22 |
| Then and now | 8 | Jesus begins his work | 24 |
| How the Bible was written | 10 | Parables and miracles | 26 |
| What Archaeologists have found | 12 | The spread of Christianity | 28 |
| The Bible today | 14 | Reading the Bible | 30 |
| People in the Bible | 16 | Bible quiz | 31 |

### Jacqueline Dineen • Illustrator Joseph McEwan

BROCKHAMPTON PRESS
LONDON

# What is the Bible?

*People often think of the Bible as one book – a sort of history book which spans more than a thousand years. In fact, the Bible is a collection of separate books written by many different people over a long period of time.*

There are sixty-two books altogether in the Bible, thirty-nine in the Old Testament and twenty-seven in the New Testament. Some of the books are based on history, but there are also stories, words of wisdom, poetry and hymns.

In a way, the Bible *is* one long story – the story of the people of Israel and the way in which they believed that God influenced their lives. The Old Testament is the name Christians have given to the Holy writings of the Jewish people. The first five books are called the Law, or the Torah in Hebrew, the language of the Jewish people. The next twelve are the History books, from the time of Moses (about 1300 BC) to the end of the Old Testament (about 400 BC). Then there are five books of wise sayings, poetry, plays and hymns. The Old Testament ends with the books of Prophets. A prophet was someone believed to have been sent by God to preach a message to the people.

The New Testament tells the story of Jesus, the son of God, and the beginning of the Christian religion.

The Bible is not only a collection of religious books, but also gives many clues about how people lived in Bible times. For many years, it was the only evidence people had that there had been life in the Bible lands two to three thousand years ago.

Today, it is a different story. Archaeologists have excavated (dug up) old cities and buildings in the Bible lands and discovered evidence about life in Bible times. We can visit the Bible lands ourselves and see what the climate and landscape are like. This helps us to imagine what life was like then.

The books of the Bible are divided up into chapters, each with a number at the beginning. The chapters are divided into verses with smaller numbers next to them. This makes it easy to find the part you want. References to verses are written like this:

**Genesis 13:8**

(the book of Genesis, chapter 13, verse 8).

# The Bible Lands

*Most of the events you can read about in the Bible took place in Israel, which is in the Near East.*

The early books of the Bible tell the story of how God chose Abraham and his family to found the nation of Israel. He told Abraham to leave the city of Ur in Mesopotamia and go to Canaan.

Canaan was a narrow strip of land between the Mediterranean Sea and the Arabian desert. The southern part later became Israel, and the northern part – modern Lebanon – became Phoenicia. The Canaanites traded with the lands around the Mediterranean, particularly Egypt.

Canaan was important because of its trading activities and also because it was a link between Africa and Asia. Travellers and merchants passed through it on their way to the great cities of the ancient world. Canaan itself did not have big cities. Separate tribes or clans built their own towns and villages. The towns were often built on a hill and had walls round them to keep out invaders.

## Fantastic Facts

GOODS WERE SOLD BY WEIGHT IN BIBLE TIMES. JEWISH COINS WERE CALLED SHEKELS. THE WORD SHEKEL MEANS 'TO WEIGH'.

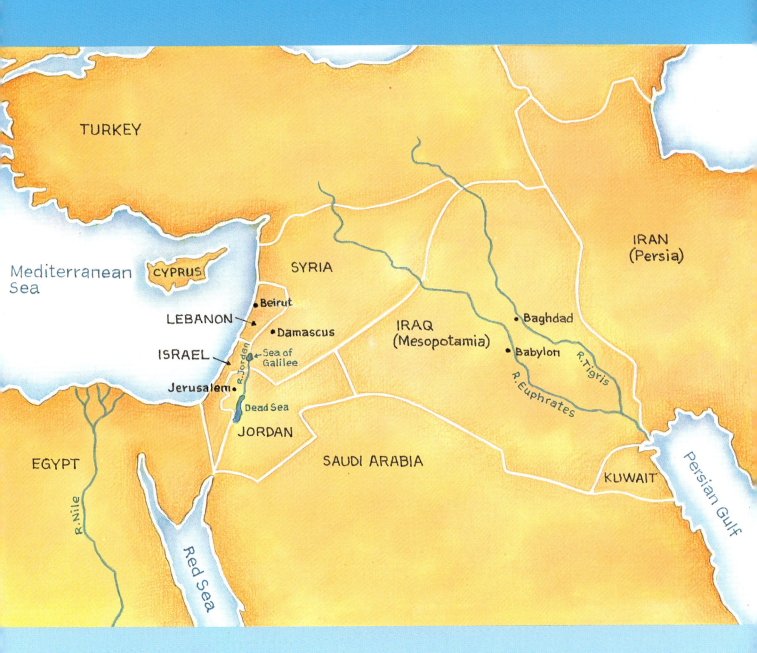

# Now you see

Other peoples lived around the Bible lands and played a part in the Bible story. The Babylonians, the Assyrians, the Egyptians, the Greeks and the Romans are some others. Can you find out more about these civilisations? Pinpoint where they lived on the map.

Imagine that you are an Egyptian merchant taking a load of **papyrus** paper to Babylon. How would you make the journey? Draw a picture strip of the different sorts of transport you would use.

Most people walked or rode on donkeys. Camels carried people and loads in the desert. Carts and wagons were pulled by oxen. Rich people rode horses or had carriages. Ships had square sails and oars.

# How people lived in Bible times

Abraham and his family were nomads who lived in tents made of goat's skin. Once the Israelites settled in Canaan, they began to live in houses as the Canaanites did.

**Fantastic Facts**

PEOPLE USED TO SHOUT THEIR NEWS TO EACH OTHER FROM THE FLAT ROOFS OF THEIR HOUSES – 'SHOUTING IT FROM THE ROOFTOPS', AS THE SAYING GOES! HAVE YOU HEARD THE SAYING 'NO PEACE FOR THE WICKED'? THAT COMES FROM THE BIBLE TOO. CAN YOU FIND ANY MORE SAYINGS WE USE TODAY THAT COME FROM THE BIBLE?

The houses were made of mud bricks and had flat roofs, where people dried fruit and grain in the sun. Many of the houses only had one room, with a raised part where the family slept on a thin mattress, which was rolled up during the day. People used the roof as an extra room and sometimes slept up there. By New Testament times, the people had learned more about building from the Greeks and the Romans. Rich people had grand houses with several rooms and a courtyard in the middle.

In Old Testament times, people built their own homes and spun and wove cloth for their clothes. Craftworkers made simple, useful objects, such as pots for water and food. By New Testament times, skills had improved and there were more builders and craftworkers in the towns.

Many of the people were farmers. The main crops they grew were wheat and barley, grapes and olives. Farmers also grew other fruit, such as figs and dates, and some vegetables, and kept sheep, goats and cattle. They had simple tools such as ploughs drawn by oxen.

Each family had its own millstones for grinding grain into flour to make bread. Food was cooked by boiling or baking it over an open fire. One method of baking bread was to put the dough on stones heated in the fire. Fish was also an important food, but meat was only eaten on special occasions.

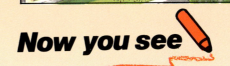

Imagine that you are preparing a meal in Bible times. What would you include? How would you cook the foods you have chosen?

# Then and now

*Some things have not changed much since Bible times.*

Tribes of nomads, the Bedouin, still move from place to place in the desert with their herds of camels. They live in tents as Abraham and his descendants did. The Bedouin wear long robes which are similar to the type of clothes people wore in Israel in Bible times. Clothing did not develop much during the whole period covered by the Bible. This was probably because of the hot climate and the lack of materials for making new types of cloth.

Poor people wore simple tunics and cloaks made of wool or goats' hair. Some flax was grown to make linen for richer people. Men and women both wore tunics. Out of doors,

*Bethlehem today*

men wore a light coat which was often brightly coloured. People had thick woollen cloaks for cold weather and wore sandals on their feet. They needed something to protect their heads from the hot sun. This was usually a square of cloth held in place by a circle of plaited wool. This type of headgear is still worn in desert regions today.

Though there are now big modern buildings in cities such as Jerusalem, some of the smaller towns look much as they would have done in Bible times, with flat-roofed houses clustered together.

Pool of Siloam

Farming is still hard because it only rains in the winter, so water has to be saved carefully. The main crops grown today are wheat, barley and citrus fruits such as oranges. There are also vines and olive trees, as there were in Bible times.

You can still see many of the places mentioned in the Bible, such as Bethlehem, Nazareth and Hebron, where Abraham lived. In Jerusalem you can see the Pool of Siloam, where Jesus sent a blind man to wash who came back able to see.

## Now you see

Make your own Bible headcloth from a towel or tea towel. You can make a headband by plaiting or twisting strands of wool or string together. Make a pair of Bible sandals by cutting feet shapes out of a piece of leather or leathercloth. Ask an adult to help you punch holes round the edge and then thread strips of leather through them.

# How the Bible was written

*Most of the Old Testament was written in Hebrew, but parts of two of the books were written in Aramaic, another ancient Jewish language.*

The books were written on long scrolls made of animal skins. Jewish scribes wrote out copies of the books from time to time, but the scrolls did not last long in the climate of the Bible lands, so very few of the original documents have been found.

The books were written by different people. No one is sure who wrote them all, or how they came together in one book, but the Jewish people believe that they were collected by the scribe Ezra. King Solomon wrote poetry and proverbs. David, the shepherd boy who became king, wrote poetry that appears in the book of Psalms. However, some books are named after the people they are about, not their author.

The New Testament was written in Greek and original documents still survive. The earliest books were probably written on scrolls of leather or papyrus. Then someone had the idea of folding the paper into a book called a **codex** which was easier to read than a long scroll. The earliest complete version of the New Testament is the *Codex Sinaiticus*.

The four Gospels tell the story of Jesus. The word Gospel means 'good news'. The Gospels were written by Matthew, a tax collector, who became one of Jesus' disciples; Mark, a young boy whose house Jesus used to visit; and Luke, a doctor. People are not sure if John's Gospel was written by another of Jesus' disciples, John, who was a fisherman.

## Fantastic Facts

THE BIBLE CONTAINS 3,566,480 LETTERS. THINK HOW LONG IT WOULD TAKE TO COPY ALL THAT OUT BY HAND!

*A modern-day scribe handwrites the bible*

## How writing began

The first form of writing was invented in Babylonia over 5,000 years ago. Words were shown by simple shapes pressed into clay tablets. This was known as **cuneiform writing.** The ancient Egyptians used picture writing called hieroglyphs. A scribe from Canaan invented an alphabet with a symbol for each consonant. For example, his word for ox began with an 'A' sound, so he drew an ox for the letter 'A'. Through time this became 'A' as we know it.

## Now you see

Make up your own way of writing by thinking of a different picture for each letter of the alphabet. Write someone a message in your alphabet and see if they can 'decode' it.

*A Hebrew scroll*

*Codex Sinaiticus*

# What archaeologists have found

Until the nineteenth century, most people reading the Bible had to imagine what life was like in the Bible lands all those centuries ago. Since then, however, archaeologists have been able to fill in some of the gaps.

Archaeologists excavate the earth to find evidence about the past. They may find the ruins of a town or city which show what buildings were like and how the streets were laid out. There may also be bits of pottery, metalwork and other examples of the ornaments and utensils people had.

*Archaeologists at work in the Bible lands*

In order to find this evidence, archaeologists have to know where to look for ancient ruins. The Bible mentions many places, and archaeologists have been able to work on some of these. In cities such as Jerusalem, where old buildings

*Excavation in Jerusalem*

*Excavations in Jericho*

have been buried under newer ones, archaeologists cannot just start digging. They have to wait until a building is being demolished, or choose an area which has no buildings on it. That is why the excavations in Jerusalem, Damascus and other cities in the Bible lands have to be carried out over a long period of time.

**The Dead Sea Scrolls**
In 1947, a shepherd boy found some jars in a cave near the Dead Sea. Inside the jars were some leather scrolls. Archaeologists investigated the caves and found more of these scrolls. There were about five hundred altogether and they were copies of all the Old Testament books except Esther. They had been the library of a religious group who lived there over 2,000 years ago. The Dead Sea Scrolls are 1,000 years older than any other copies of the Old Testament that have been found.

Artefacts found in Bible land excavations

The Dead Sea Scrolls

## Now you see

Ask an adult if you can carry out your own archaeological 'dig' in part of your garden. You may find toys or bits of china that give you clues about the people who lived there before!

The caves where the Dead Sea Scrolls were discovered

# The Bible today

The first Christians travelled around the Bible lands and parts of Europe, telling people about the teachings of Jesus.

They took copies of the Old Testament and later the Gospels and letters written by Christian leaders, and translated them into the languages of the different people they met. The first translation of the Bible was from Greek to Latin, which was the official language of the Roman Empire. The final list of books to be included in the New Testament was agreed by two church councils, one at Laodicea in AD 363 and the other at Carthage in AD 397.

It was confusing to have many different translations and in AD 384, Pope Damasus instructed his secretary, Jerome, to make the official Latin translation. This was known as the 'Vulgate' (or 'everyday') Bible.

Before printing was invented in the fifteenth century, all book manuscripts had to be copied by hand. Many were copied by monks who often decorated them with gold, silver and brilliant colours. These were known as **illuminated manuscripts.** They were very expensive and few people could afford them.

The printing press was invented by Johann Gutenberg at Mainz in Germany in about 1450. His first printed book, the Gutenberg Bible, appeared in 1456.

As the Roman Empire crumbled, Latin died out as the main spoken language. Only priests and scholars could read the Latin Bible, so people set about translating it into other languages. An Oxford scholar, John Wycliffe, had it translated into English in the fourteenth century. Another scholar, William Tyndale, made a much better translation about one hundred years later.

Many English versions of the Bible have appeared since. The older versions can be difficult to understand. The most modern ones, such as *The New International Version* and *The Good News Bible*, aim to make the meaning clearer by writing in everyday language.

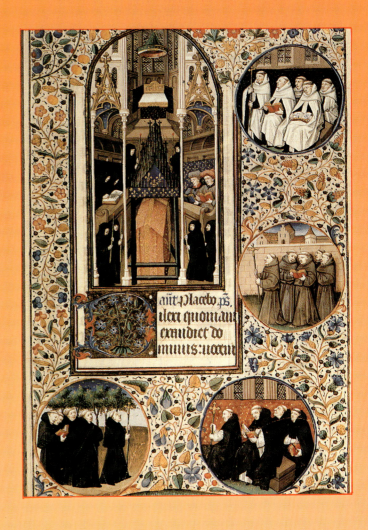

## Now you see

These illuminated letters show the sort of designs the monks used. Draw your own illuminated letters and paint or colour them.

### Fantastic Facts

THE FIRST TRANSLATION OF THE BIBLE TO APPEAR IN ENGLAND WAS BISHOP ALDHELM'S TRANSLATION OF THE PSALMS IN AD 700. THE MONK BEDE BEGAN TO TRANSLATE THE BIBLE INTO ANGLO-SAXON AT ABOUT THE SAME TIME BUT HE DIED BEFORE HE HAD FINISHED IT.

By 1456 Gutenberg had printed the Vulgate version of the Bible

# People in the Bible

*The Bible is full of stories that show us how people thought and their beliefs about God.*

**Moses**
The Bible tells us that Abraham and his family went to Canaan from Ur as God had told them to. Abraham's grandson, Jacob, had twelve sons. One of his sons, Joseph, was sold as a slave to an officer in Egypt. God warned Joseph that there would be a famine and Jacob sent his other sons to Egypt. These twelve men founded the twelve tribes which became the Israelites.

The Israelites became so strong and powerful that the king, or Pharaoh, of Egypt was afraid of them and made them his slaves. He ordered that every Israelite baby boy should be killed.

One Israelite woman hid her baby in the bullrushes by the river, where the Pharaoh's daughter found him. The baby, Moses, grew up in the Pharaoh's palace.

Moses became the leader of the Israelites and led them out of Egypt to freedom. They journeyed through the desert to Mount Sinai, where God appeared to Moses and his brother Aaron and gave him ten laws that the people must obey. The laws, which are known as the **Ten Commandments**, were written on stone tablets. God told Moses to build him a special tent called a tabernacle. The stone tablets were to be put into a **covenant** (agreement) box, called the Ark of the Covenant, and kept in the tabernacle.

The Israelites continued their journey to the borders of Canaan, but they were afraid of being attacked by the Canaanites. God was angry because they did not trust him and sent them to wander in the desert for forty years. When Moses died, God chose Joshua to lead the people back to Canaan and conquer the city of Jericho.

### Now you see

The Bible gives a detailed description of the tabernacle and the Ark of the Covenant in the book of Exodus. Read about it and draw a picture of what you think it looked like.

### Fantastic Facts

GOD TOLD THE PEOPLE TO WORK FOR SIX DAYS AND REST ON SATURDAY, THE SABBATH. THE JEWS STILL KEEP SATURDAY AS THE SABBATH, BUT CHRISTIANS KEEP SUNDAY AS THEIR DAY OF REST BECAUSE THEY BELIEVE THAT JESUS ROSE FROM THE DEAD ON SUNDAY.

# Two famous kings

*The Israelites conquered the Canaanites and Canaan became known as Israel.*

During the next two hundred years, the people were led by military heroes, the **Judges**. The Israelites were often at war with the Philistines, who lived to the south-west of Israel. Samuel was the last and greatest of the Judges. When he grew old, the people asked him to give them a king as other nations had.

The first king was Saul, but the Bible says that God was not pleased with him because he grew proud and disobeyed God. So God chose a shepherd boy, David, as the next king.

David spent his days minding his father's sheep on the hillsides near Bethlehem. Three of his brothers were in Saul's army which was once again fighting the Philistines. One of the Philistines was a giant of a man called Goliath.

One day, David was sent with food for his brothers. He heard Goliath challenging the Israelites to send someone out to fight him, and he decided that he would accept the giant's challenge. He took his sling and five smooth stones. Goliath jeered when he saw the boy, but David aimed a stone which hit Goliath on the forehead and killed him.

When Saul died, David became king. At first, he ruled over Judah in the South, but he gradually gained control of the whole of Israel. Then he defeated enemies such as the Ammonites and extended his kingdom even further. He made Jerusalem his capital city.

David's son, Solomon, was the next king. He built a magnificent temple for God in Jerusalem. Solomon loved beautiful things and imposed heavy taxes on the people so that he could put fine buildings in the capital.

### Fantastic Facts

THE BIBLE SAYS GOD TOLD SOLOMON THAT HE WOULD GIVE HIM GREAT WISDOM. WE STILL USE THE SAYING 'THE WISDOM OF SOLOMON' TODAY.

## Now you see

Digits, palms, spans and cubits were measurements of length in Bible times. Goliath was 6 cubits and a span tall. Measure an adult's arm to find out how tall he was. A donkey-load was a measure of capacity. It equalled 220 litres.

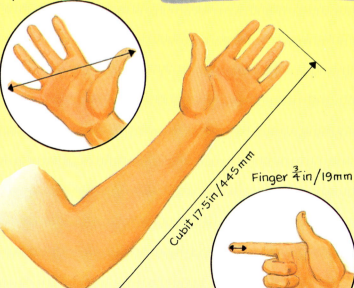

Span 9in / 230mm

Cubit 17.5in / 445mm

Finger 3/4 in / 19mm

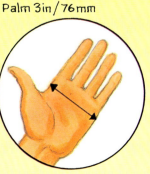

Palm 3in / 76mm

# The books of wisdom

*The books of Job, Psalms and Proverbs contain stories, popular sayings and common-sense rules for living a good life.*

We do not know who wrote the book of Job. Most of it is written in poetry. It is about a wealthy and very good man, Job, who is struck by terrible disasters. He loses all his children and his possessions and is struck down by disease. Job, and three friends who come to see him, cannot understand why he is being made to suffer so much when he has led such a good life. Then God appears to Job and asks him why he is questioning his actions. Job recognises that he is the almighty and feels humble. God gives him back his health and his money and possessions. Another well-known saying, 'he has the patience of Job', stems from this story.

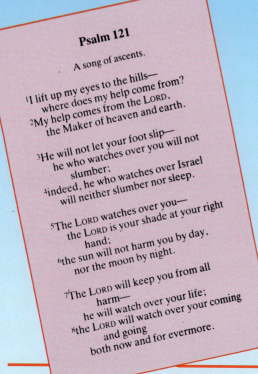

**Psalm 121**

A song of ascents.

¹I lift up my eyes to the hills—
where does my help come from?
²My help comes from the LORD,
the Maker of heaven and earth.

³He will not let your foot slip—
he who watches over you will not slumber;
⁴indeed, he who watches over Israel
will neither slumber nor sleep.

⁵The LORD watches over you—
the LORD is your shade at your right hand;
⁶the sun will not harm you by day,
nor the moon by night.

⁷The LORD will keep you from all harm—
he will watch over your life;
⁸the LORD will watch over your coming and going
both now and for evermore.

The Book of Psalms is a collection of poems, hymns and prayers. They were written by many different people over many years and were read or chanted during ceremonies of worship. Some of them ask for God's help or forgiveness, others thank him for what he has done for the people. King David loved music and wrote many hymns which appear in the Book of Psalms.

A **proverb** is a short saying, such as 'a change is as good as a rest' or 'a rolling stone gathers no moss', which sums up something that is true about life. What do you think these two proverbs mean, for example? Many of the proverbs we use today have been changed to make the meaning clearer, or were made up later than the Bible proverbs. But if you look at the books of Proverbs in the Bible, you can recognise some of the sayings we still use today. For example, Proverbs 16:18 'Pride goes before destruction, a haughty spirit before a fall'. Today we know that as 'Pride goes before a fall'. And Proverbs 14:24 'He who spares the rod hates his son' has become 'Spare the rod and spoil the child'.

It is said that Solomon wrote more than 3,000 proverbs. The Queen of Sheba visited him to test his wisdom.

## Now you see

Match these two halves of a sentence to make some well-known proverbs.
Never look a gift . . .          . . . out of a sow's ear
All that glitters . . .          . . . never boils
You can't make a silk purse . . .   . . . is not gold
A watched pot . . .          . . . horse in the mouth

21

# The prophets

*There are seventeen books of Prophets and most of them are named after the prophet they are about.*

People believed that the prophets were sent by God to teach them and warn them about things that would happen if they were greedy or did wrong.

The prophet Isaiah lived in Jerusalem in the eighth century BC. At the time, the province of Judah was under threat from the Assyrians who had a great empire. Isaiah warned the people that they had not trusted God and had disobeyed him. He said they must love God and he would protect them against the Assyrians. Seven years later, the Assyrians marched to the gates of Jerusalem. The Assyrian king wrote to King Hezekiah of Judah, saying that he would destroy the city. Hezekiah went to the Temple and asked God to help his people. That night, thousands of soldiers died in the Assyrian camp. No one knew why. After that, the King of Assyria left Jerusalem in peace.

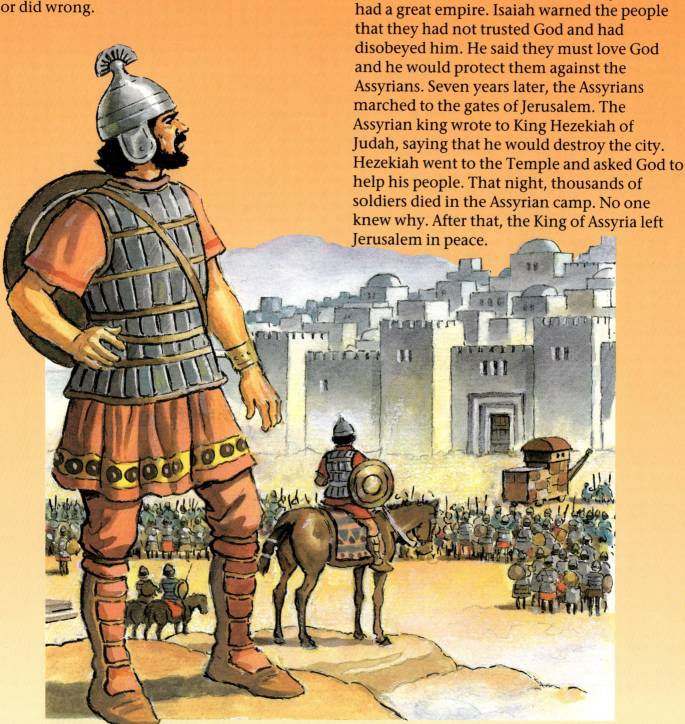

Then Isaiah warned Hezekiah that one day the Babylonians would take many people captive. He said that many years later, God would send a child who would be the ruler of the people.

After Hezekiah, there were some bad kings who did not worship God. The people became cruel and selfish. Another prophet, Jeremiah, tried to warn them that their behaviour would destroy them. But the people did not listen. King Nebuchadnezzar of Babylon took control of Judah and many Jews were captured and taken to Babylon. The prophet Ezekiel was one of the prisoners and he worked among the Jewish people in Babylon. He predicted that Jerusalem would be captured and the Temple destroyed. Then news came that Nebuchadnezzar had destroyed Jerusalem. The people were in despair, but Ezekiel promised that God would save the people and bring them back home one day.

## Now you see

Jonah was a prophet who disobeyed God. Read about him and make a picture strip story using these captions.

1. God told Jonah to go to Assyria but he disobeyed. He caught a ship for Spain. God was angry and sent a big storm.
2. Jonah said, 'Throw me overboard and God will stop the storm'.
3. The sea grew calm but a big fish swallowed Jonah alive.
4. Jonah told God he was sorry.
5. God made the fish throw Jonah out.

## Fantastic Facts

ANOTHER WELL-KNOWN SAYING, 'A WOLF IN SHEEP'S CLOTHING', COMES FROM WHAT JESUS SAID ABOUT FALSE PROPHETS. 'WATCH OUT FOR FALSE PROPHETS. THEY COME TO YOU IN SHEEP'S CLOTHING BUT INWARDLY THEY ARE FEROCIOUS WOLVES.' WHAT DO YOU THINK THIS MEANS?

# Jesus begins his work

*The people finally returned from exile when Babylon became part of the Persian empire and the Persian king, Cyrus, gave them their freedom.*

Hundreds of years passed, during which the Persian empire fell to Alexander the Great of Greece and Israel came under Greek influence. By the time Jesus was born, the Romans had conquered the Greeks and taken control. They appointed their own king, Herod. The people hated Herod because he was cruel, and they longed for freedom from the Romans. They remembered that the prophets had said God would send a King and they imagined a soldier king who would drive the Romans out. So when Jesus was born, many people did not realise who he was.

The four Gospels tell us about Jesus and the work he did. He grew up in the town of Nazareth, which is in Galilee in the north of Israel. His father, Joseph, was a carpenter and when Jesus grew up he began working in his shop. But he knew that it was almost time to begin the work he had been sent for by God.

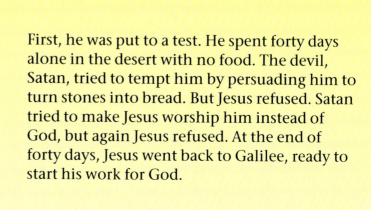

First, he was put to a test. He spent forty days alone in the desert with no food. The devil, Satan, tried to tempt him by persuading him to turn stones into bread. But Jesus refused. Satan tried to make Jesus worship him instead of God, but again Jesus refused. At the end of forty days, Jesus went back to Galilee, ready to start his work for God.

He began to preach in Nazareth, but people would not listen. They did not believe a carpenter could have anything to teach them. So he went to nearby towns and villages where people would listen.

As Jesus travelled around, he collected his twelve **disciples**, or followers, who went with him. Andrew, Simon (whom Jesus called Peter), James and John were fisherman on Lake Galilee. The other eight were Matthew (the tax collector), Philip, Bartholomew, Thomas, James, Simon, Judas, and Judas Iscariot.

## Now you see

*Make a stained glass window. Draw a design on a piece of card and cut out the shapes. Stick coloured tissue paper behind each shape. Stick your card on a window so that the light shines through. You could make your window for Christmas or Easter.*

25

# Parables and miracles

*Jesus talked to the people about God and the sort of life he expected them to lead.*

Sometimes the people found it hard to understand what Jesus was saying, so he used stories called **parables** to show what he meant. He told this parable about being a good neighbour:

A man was travelling along the road from Jerusalem to Jericho when he was attacked by bandits. They beat him up, robbed him and left him lying there. After a while a priest came along. He saw the man but he did not help him. He walked past on the other side of the road. Then a preacher came along but he did not help the man either.

Then a Samaritan came along the road. He took pity on the man, and washed and bandaged his wounds. He put him on his own donkey and took him to an inn. The next day he had to leave but he gave the innkeeper some money and said, 'Look after him. If it costs more than this, I will pay you when I come back.' Jesus asked, 'Which of these people was a good neighbour?'

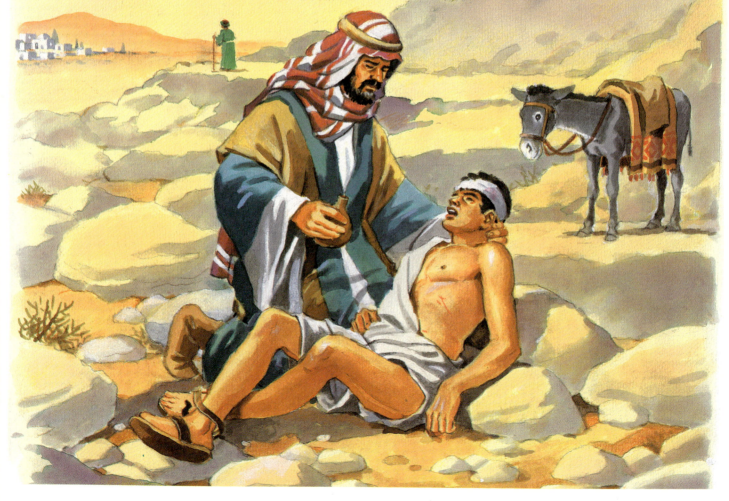

The people were amazed by the miracles that Jesus could perform. News spread about the illnesses he could cure and people came from far and wide to be healed. One day, an official named Jairus came to Jesus and asked him to heal his twelve-year-old daughter who was dying. Jesus went with him but when they reached Jairus's house, his daughter had died and all the people were wailing. Jesus told them that the girl was not dead, but asleep. The people laughed at him because they knew she was dead. Jesus took her hand and said, 'My child, get up,' and she stood up at once.

## Now you see

Read some of the parables Jesus told and then make up a modern parable about life today. Jesus performed other miracles besides healing people. Read about the feeding of the five thousand and paint a picture of the story.

### Fantastic Facts

THE SHORTEST VERSE IN THE BIBLE IS JOHN 11:35. IT SAYS 'JESUS WEPT'.

# The spread of Christianity

*Crowds followed Jesus and listened to his teachings, but he was not popular with everyone.*

The **Pharisees** were a strict religious group who were shocked when Jesus healed people on the Sabbath. The priests were angry when Jesus went to the Temple in Jerusalem and threw out money-changers and people who were selling doves. Jesus said they had made the Temple 'a den of robbers'.

The four Gospels are followed by the Acts which tells how the disciples carried on preaching to the people. On the Day of Pentecost, a Jewish festival, Peter spoke to the crowds about Jesus. That day, 3,000 people became Christians.

The priests wanted to arrest Jesus and kill him. One of his disciples, Judas Iscariot, went to the priests and said he would lead them to Jesus when there was no one about. The priests paid Judas thirty silver coins.

Jesus was captured in the Garden of Gethsemane by guards and priests led by Judas. He was sentenced to death and crucified. The next day, his friends found that his body was not in its tomb. Later, they came to believe that Jesus was still alive and with them, and that he had risen from the dead. This is called the resurrection.

Many people who flocked to hear the disciples became Christians. This angered the priests and the Pharisees. One Pharisee, a young man called Paul, was determined to get rid of the Christians. Some were thrown into prisons. Others escaped to other countries where they carried on their preaching.

Paul went to Damascus in Syria because he had heard there were Christians there. On the way, he was blinded by a bright light and heard Jesus's voice. His companions led him into Damascus where a Christian called Ananias laid his hands on Paul and gave him back his sight. From then on, Paul stopped fighting the Christians and became one of them. He spent his life travelling around the Mediterranean lands, telling everyone about Jesus and converting more people to Christianity.

## Now you see

Make a Bible bookmark. On one side, draw a picture of your favourite story and on the other side make a list of the passages you like and where to find them in your Bible.

*The journeys of St Paul, as described in the Book of Acts.*

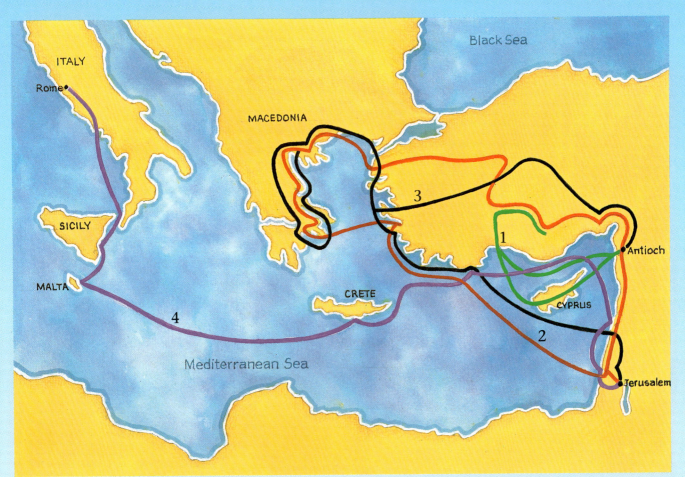

# Reading the Bible

*You have read a few stories from the Bible in this book but there are many more. If you haven't read the Bible, or got a copy of it, it can be difficult to know where to start.*

The first step is to buy a Bible or book of Bible stories which you can understand and enjoy. There are children's versions of the *New International Version* and the *Good News Bible* and several books which pick out a selection of stories from the Bible.

You could start by reading some well-known stories about Jesus from the four Gospels. If your Bible has a list of Bible stories and where to find them, pick out some famous ones like Noah's Ark (Genesis), Moses crossing the Red Sea (Exodus), Joshua and the Battle of Jericho (Joshua), or David and Goliath (Samuel) to start you off.

Remember that the Bible is not just a collection of stories. It was written to teach people about God. So you have to ask whether it is telling a story, or giving words of wisdom. Is it poetry or prose? Does it have a special meaning or message for people?

# Bible quiz

1. What is the first book of the Bible?
2. What does the word 'gospel' mean?
3. Why do Christians keep Sunday as their day of rest?
4. Who was a very patient man?
5. Who was a very wise man?
6. Which writer was a tax collector?
7. Which of the disciples were fishermen?
8. Who invented the printing press?
9. Who completed the first English translation of the Bible?
10. What languages was the Bible first written in?
11. Which king loved music?
12. Which king asked God for help against the Assyrians?
13. What type of stories did Jesus tell?
14. Who invented the first type of writing?
15. Where did Moses receive the Ten Commandments?
16. Name three prophets mentioned in this book.
17. Why do you think David carried a sling?
18. Whose army was Goliath with?
19. Who was a good neighbour?
20. How many books are there in the Bible?

**Answers to proverbs on page 21**
Never look a gift horse in the mouth.
All that glitters is not gold.
You can't make a silk purse out of a sow's ear.
A watched pot never boils.

**Answers to quiz**
1. Genesis.
2. Good news.
3. Because they believe that Jesus rose from the dead on Sunday.
4. Job
5. Solomon
6. Matthew
7. Andrew, Simon (Peter), James and John
8. Johann Gutenberg
9. John Wycliffe
10. Hebrew, Aramaic (Old Testament), Greek (New Testament)
11. David
12. Hezekiah
13. Parables
14. The Babylonians
15. Mount Sinai
16. Isaiah, Jeremiah, Ezekiel, Jonah
17. To fend off wild animals that tried to attack his sheep
18. The Philistines
19. The Good Samaritan
20. 66

# Index

Abraham 4, 6, 9, 16
Aldhelm, Bishop 15
alphabets 11
Ananias 29
archaeology 3, 12-13
Ark of the Covenant 16
artefacts 12, 13
Assyrians 5, 22

Babylon 23
Baylonians 5, 23
Bede 15
Bedouin 8
Bethlehem 8, 9

Canaan 4, 6, 14-15
Carthage 14
cloth 7
clothing 8-9
Christianity 2, 14, 28-29
codex 10-11
*Codex sinaiticus* 10
cooking 7
crafts 7
crucifixion 28
cuneiform writing 11

Damascus 13, 29
Damasus, Pope 14
David 18-19, 20
Dead Sea Scrolls 13
disciples 25

Egyptians 5, 16
Ezekiel 23

farming 7, 9
food 7

Goliath 18
*Good News Bible* 15, 30
Good Samaritan 27
Gospels 10, 24
Greeks 5, 7, 24
Gutenberg, Johann 15

Hebron 9
Herod 24
Hezekiah 22-23
hieroglyphs 11
History books 2
houses 7

illuminated manuscripts 14-15
Isaiah 22-23
Israelites 6, 16-17, 18-19

Jairus's daughter 27
Jericho 12
Jerome 14
Jerusalem 9, 12-13, 19, 22-23
Jesus 2, 10, 14, 23, 24-29
Job 20
John 10
Jonah 23
Joshua 17
Judas Iscariot 28
Judges 18

Latin Bible 14-15
Laodicea 14
Law books 2
Luke 10

Mark 10
Matthew 10
measurements 19
miracles 27

Moses 2, 16-17

Nazareth 9, 24, 25
Nebuchadnezzar 23
*New International Version* 15, 30
New Testament 2-3, 10
nomads 6-8

Old Testament 2-3, 10, 13

papyrus 5
parables 26
Paul 29
Persians 24
Peter 28
Pharisees 28-9
Philistines 18
Pool of Siloam 9
printing 15
Prophets 2, 22-23
Proverbs 21
Psalms 20

Romans 5, 7, 14-15, 24

Satan 24
Saul 18-19
scribes 10
scrolls 10
Solomon 18-19, 21

Ten Commandments 16
Torah 2
towns 4, 9
trade 4-5
transport 5
Tyndale, William 15

Vulgate Bible 14-15

writing 11
Wycliffe, John 15

**British Library Catalogue in Publication Data**
A catalogue for this book is available from the British Library.
ISBN 1-86019-539-3
First published 1993
© 1993 Jacqueline Dineen
This edition published 1997 by Brockhampton Press, a member of Hodder Headline PLC Group.
10 9 8 7 6 5 4 3 2 1
1999 1998 1997

All rights reserved. No part of this publication may be reproduced or transmitted in any form or by any means, electronic or mechanical, including photocopy, recording, or any information storage and retrieval system, without permission in writing from the publisher or under licence from the Copyright Licensing Agency Limited. Further details of such licences (for reprographic reproduction) may be obtained from the Copyright Licensing Agency Limited, of 90 Tottenham Court Road, London W1P 9HE.

Typeset by Litho Link Ltd, Welshpool, Powys, Wales.
Printed in India.

The author and publishers would like to thank the following for permission to reproduce photographic material in this book:

Andes Press Agency p.21; Barnaby's Picture Library p.13; J. Allan Cash Ltd. p. 3, 8, 10, 12, 13; Robert Harding Picture Library p.10, 12, 13; Sonia Halliday Photographs p.11, 15; The Jewish Museum p.11; The Mansell Collection p.15; Trinity College, Cambridge p.14.